Not Your Average
Adult

Navigating Adulthood with Jesus

FRANCESCA CAMPBELL

WESTBOW
PRESS®
A DIVISION OF THOMAS NELSON
& ZONDERVAN

WestBow Press books may be ordered through booksellers or by contacting:

WestBow Press
A Division of Thomas Nelson & Zondervan
1663 Liberty Drive
Bloomington, IN 47403
www.westbowpress.com
844-714-3454

Scripture quotations taken from The Holy Bible, New International
Version® NIV® Copyright © 1973 1978 1984 2011 by Biblica,
Inc. TM. Used by permission. All rights reserved worldwide.

ISBN: 979-8-3850-2957-0 (sc)
ISBN: 979-8-3850-2958-7 (e)

Library of Congress Control Number: 2024914487

Print information available on the last page.

WestBow Press rev. date: 08/13/2024

CONTENTS

A Note to the Reader

When I was studying to get my bachelors degree I would spend time between classes doing homework at Starbucks or doing a little shopping. One of my favorite places to shop at was Life Way. I was always looking for new Bible studies or curriculum for the teens in my youth group at church. One day I went in looking for a devotional for myself. All I could find that day were devotionals for married women, mothers, or teenage girls. I found nothing that fit me: a single, young, college student. So, I left and told myself I would just write my own. From that day on, I set up shop at Starbucks twice a week between my college classes and started writing.

When I graduated with my Bachelor's degree, I stopped writing. I knew I wasn't done with it but my life got busier. After I graduated with my Master's degree, I revisited the book. I enjoy writing and studying what the Bible says about topics I was struggling with as a young adult. When God told me to share it with others, I was scared. I never intended to share this with anyone. It was something fun for me to pour into and talk to God about. But I want to be obedient to Him.

I hope that as you read this, no matter what season of life you are in, you feel seen. Know that the things you might be experiencing in this season of your life are normal. Becoming an adult is hard. Society makes it even harder for Christians. If you are like me or the other young adults in my life, entering adulthood can be so busy, tiring and overwhelming. It can also be exciting and fun! This book is not meant to be hard. I hope, as you read this, that you begin to feel confident enough to be more than average. "What does that mean? It means to stand out and let the fruits of your relationship with God shine. Chase after God's path for your life and give Him everything.

Am I An Adult Yet?

What really qualifies someone to be an "adult"? After all, there's no special test or even a manual. Is being an adult a classification that we just receive once we turn a certain age? How do we know? I remember getting a taste of "real" adulthood when I started my first job as a senior in high school. It made me feel closer to adulthood–not because I was making my own money, but because I had to start taking responsibility. Even still in my mid 20's, I have a habit of "rewarding myself" when I do something I think is "adulting." For example, get the oil changed in my car: go to Starbucks. Go to the bank: go shopping. This sounds fun, but "adulting" is so much more.

> **"Do not conform to the pattern of this world,**
> **but be transformed by the renewing of your mind.**
> **Then you will be able to test and**
> **approve what God's will is–**
> **His good, pleasing and perfect will."**
> **Romans 12:2**

I love this verse! Entering adulthood, I was faced with many opportunities, good and bad. I had to take responsibility for my actions, decisions, finances, and my future. I had to start doing things for ME and had the realization that <u>no one</u> was going to do life for me. To me, being a "real adult" started with taking responsibility for who I am and what I want to be, including taking ownership of my relationship with the Lord. Sometimes, when I think of all my responsibilities, I am frightened that I am not making the right choices. But that is why I love this verse so much! It gives me the reassurance that if I make God's intentions my own, His will for my life will never fail. There is nothing I can do to hinder God's plan for my life. As I navigate this thing called "adulting" this one thing remains: Seek God above all.

One day, I was video messaging my friend and telling her that I ran a bunch of errands that day and was rewarding myself with Starbucks for "adulting." She said, "Francesca, you're 25. I don't think you can say you're "adulting" anymore." I laughed (as to not cry a little), but she opened my eyes more than she realized. All of that to say, it gets easier, friends. The oil changes, the paying bills, the important phone calls…it gets easier the more you practice. How do you get through "adulting"? Let God guide your steps, guide your decisions, and give you the courage (and patience) you need to be an "adult." My challenge to you? Don't be your average adult. Let God mold you into the "adult" He created you to be.

It is time to take responsibility.
What are some things you need to take
responsibility for now in this stage of your life?

Too Many Expectations

The first sign that I was becoming a "new" adult was when all the questions were asked: "Where are you going to college?," "Do you know what you're going to be?," "Where are you going to live?," "Do you have a job yet?," or "Are you dating anyone?" It just makes me want to yell "STOP!" This all started when I was a junior in high school, where the thoughts of adulthood and my future scared me half to death, and it only got worse as I graduated. All around me were the expectations from my friends and family, the world and... myself.

"Call to me and I will answer you
and tell you great and unsearchable things
you do not know."
Jeremiah 33:3

Can you breathe again? Oftentimes, the answer to these expectations is "I don't know." That's okay. It is okay to not know what to do next. The way we judge our own expectations and the ones from others and how we balance them speaks a great deal of our trust in Jesus Christ. Our expectations may not even be achievable; they could be the very thing that is holding us back from our true calling. When we call upon the Lord in every aspect of our lives, He will show up. We don't have to go through life in any stage alone.

So what does God expect from us? What are the expectations we should be striving for? The best piece of advice I've ever been given was: "Do your best, and that's good enough." My dad told me that as a young middle school-aged girl, and I still live by that advice today. God desires our heart and a relationship with Him. Once we repent and give our lives to Him, we are expected to live according to His word. So as we are dealing with expectations from the world (including from ourselves), we can ask ourselves these things: "Does it align with God's Word?" and "Am I seeking God's will above everything else?" Sometimes, giving God our best means letting go of the expectations we are holding onto so tightly. Sometimes, giving God our best may feel less than. However, when our heart's desire is in alignment with His Word, that is good enough. I might add to my dad's advice and say, "Do your best, and let God handle the rest." And remember, His plan and timeline are always greater than our own.

What expectations do you have for yourself?
What do you think God's expectations are from you?

What To Do When You Don't Know What To Do

Do you ever just feel like your life is flashing before your eyes? Deadlines are approaching, decisions have to be made, or things you put off are now staring you in the face. Maybe you feel like your life is at a standstill. You are ready for the next chapter in your life, but here's the catch: you don't know what that next chapter is. You feel restless. What do you do when you don't know what to do?

Amongst the frustration of not knowing what to do, we often ask: "God, where are You?" Whether we are waiting for an answer or a sign from God to guide us, our patience seems quite thin as we play the waiting game.

> **"I remain confident of this:**
> **I will see the goodness of the Lord**
> **in the land of the living.**
> **Wait for the Lord;**
> **be strong and take heart**
> **and wait for the Lord."**
> **Psalm 27:13-14**

God's silence does not mean God's absence. In the moments when you feel as though your world is spinning and you have no answers, trust that God knows what He is doing. Remember to see the goodness in what God has done for you in the past, and have hope in the goodness He has in store for you in the future. As we are waiting and trusting in the Lord to reveal Himself to us, remember to believe that God knows what is best for us. He will never give us something we can't handle without Him. In my experience, there is always something to be learned in the waiting. What is God teaching you as you wait to see what He wants you to do next? Is it patience, growth in your faith, reliance completely on Him?

What then do we do when it's time to make a decision about our next steps, but we still don't feel like God has given us a clear answer? One could say that when we are waiting for direction from God, we are also waiting to hear His voice. What we tend to forget is that God speaks in ways other than verbally to us. The Bible is God's Word. He spoke it, and it remains true and relevant now. Are your plans, hopes, wants in alignment with what the BIble says? That's what we should be striving for as Christians. God also speaks to us through other believers. Find someone you trust, and ask them for Godly wisdom as you are trying to figure out what to do when you don't know what to do. Lastly, sometimes in order to hear from God, we must be slow to speak and quick to listen.

Think about a time when you trusted in the
Lord and He answered your prayers.
What can you learn during your time of waiting?

recently walked through a season with the Lord like never before. For a solid month or two I was hearing from God so boldly, clearly, and all the time. Almost every day, God was telling me something distinctly. Most of the time, God was telling me to give up something. Sometimes, He would tell me to do something. God was stripping things from me and revealing things to me that I didn't even realize I needed to get out of my life. Without going into all the details (because that would take a long time), God asked me to give up things like shopping, leading worship on Sunday mornings, watching certain shows and movies, unfollowing certain people on social media, my coffee table - yes, He asked me to give up my coffee table, and much, much more. MAN! was this a wild time. It was amazing hearing from God so much and so clearly, but, wow, did He convict me, mold me, and grow me. In the revelation, I was transformed and learned so much about God and myself, and iIt all started with an act of obedience.

**"Jesus replied, 'Anyone who loves me
will obey my teaching. My Father
will love them, and we will come to them
and make our home with them.'"
John 14:23**

My act of obedience was getting baptized. I had been a Christian for years and was baptized as a baby in the Methodist church, but God told me to get baptized, so I did. It was so very special. Obedience is hard yet can be simple. Let me explain my thoughts here. If God tells you to do something the answer is simple: obey. Where it is hard is 1. knowing what God is telling you to do and 2. doing something God told you to do that you really may not want to do or give up.

The more I said "yes," the more He spoke to me. Sometimes, it was scary, but the freedom that came with obeying the Lord was indescribable. This is also practicing faith. Oftentimes, obeying the Lord means stepping out in faith. Here's the thing: we don't always know why God tells us to do something, but that doesn't matter. We aren't the potter, we are the clay. We don't have to understand the why in order to obey. Obedience to God is submission to His will. It's sacrifice. It's willingness to His way over our way. It's THE WAY. Obedience is necessary in our walk with God. As Jesus said in John, if we love Him, we will keep His word. Proverbs 8:32 says, "...blessed are those who keep my ways." We shouldn't obey just to be blessed by God, but know that He rewards those who do so because they love Him. A pastor at my church once said something like this, "We can't expect God to show us our next steps if we won't do the last thing He told us to do." Punch in the gut right?

Is there something God is telling you to do?
What is keeping you from obeying Him?
Think about a time you did obey
God. What happened next?

His Voice

Thinking of God's power overwhelms me. I can recall and tell so many stories of how I've seen God's power, but, in all the times God's power has reigned in my life, the root of it all starts with His voice. There is power in His voice. Remember when I shared about the season I walked with God and I heard His voice so boldly and clearly over and over? One of the things He told me to do was during a Sunday morning. During worship that morning, He told me to go to the altar. I didn't want to. God did not stop! As God "yelled" at me to go to the altar, my body shook because His power was not to be ignored. The best way to describe His "yelling" at me is that it sounded like what I imagine Mama Francesca's voice will sound like when my child is stubbornly misbehaving. All He kept saying was "GO." I went to the altar. I surrendered everything. I am so glad He yelled at me.

Here's the thing…God doesn't always "yell" at me each time He speaks to me. Often, His voice comes as a whisper. So how do we hear God's voice? Sometimes, His voice does come as a sound, but other times, it's a feeling: a feeling of peace and His presence. Sometimes, that feeling is very obvious, but oftentimes, it is not as recognizable. So, what do we do? What do we do when we are trying to hear God's voice?

Frequently, we need to shut up. This can mean to literally be quiet, but what it also means is we need to humble ourselves before God. My pastor once said that "power is found in submission." I could talk so much about humility and submission, but here's what I mean in relation to hearing God's voice.

"Trust in the Lord with all your heart
and lean not on your own understanding;
in all your ways submit to Him,
and He will make your paths straight."
Proverbs 3:5-6

It's not about you. We must humble ourselves and realize that His way is the only way. Our ideas and plans are nothing compared to His plan for us. What does that look like? How can we expect to hear from God if we won't give up control? If we want to hear from God, we have to practice submission and listening. How? By acknowledging His presence. Acknowledging His presence is a state of mind. It is a state of constant worship. We must show up and wake up expecting the Lord. The more we make it a habit and a life shift to surrender to God and expect His presence, the more we can hear and recognize His voice. Practice, practice, practice. What do you do when you hear God's voice? Obey. Not a partial yes, but a radical obedience.

Has there been a time in your life
when you heard God's voice?
Is it easy or difficult to know if God is speaking to you?
If you are not sure if it is God's voice or your
own; ask these questions: Does it align with
the Bible? Have I talked to my mentor?

Mentorship 101

Before we got married, my husband and I went to a Dave Ramsey Financial Peace class at our church. Wow, what an eye opener! It was led by a couple from our church at the time who were also the parents of one of the teens in our youth group. During that season of our life, they were our go-to people for advice on all things "adulting." They were so supportive and encouraging, had lots of wisdom, and–most importantly–they didn't judge us for our silly adulting mistakes or that we hardly knew anything about adult life.

At the church where we are at now, I am surrounded by incredible women of God. There are so many of them that God uses to pour into my life. I have a mentor now who shows me so much love and kindness while giving me Christ-like direction. I had never really asked someone to be my mentor before, so when I approached her about being that person for me, she asked me what my expectations were. I wasn't 100% sure at the time, but knew I just needed someone to check in on me every once in a while and be there when I needed prayer or advice. She has easily become one of my favorite people. I know I can go to her for anything and she will always greet me with a big smile, warm hug, and open heart.

My husband is also surrounded by a brotherhood of Godly men at our church. I have never seen men come together in the name of Jesus like this before. They talk about real life and what the Bible says about being a man. They teach each other, grow with one another, and encourage each other. I have gotten to watch my husband grow more because of the mentor relationships he has made with several of these men at church. And many of these men's wives and children have quickly become like family.

A year after I graduated high school, I started to become closer to this girl that used to be on my school's volleyball team with me. She is only two years younger than I am, but we are in completely different stages in our lives. At that time, we would hang out, but she would talk about high school drama, boys, and things I just no longer really had an interest in. I would simply sit and listen and lend my advice if she asked for it (or if I felt a push from the Holy Spirit to do so even when she didn't ask for it). Now, as we are a little older, God is moving within her and our friendship. It is such a spirit-filled friendship that is truly life-giving to me. We have such great memories together including her being a bridesmaid in my wedding.

"As iron sharpens iron, so one person sharpens another."
Proverbs 27:17

I tell each of these tid-bits because they all have something in common. Somebody in each story is a **mentor**. Just as iron sharpens iron, it is important to have someone to help sharpen you. Having someone in your life that you can look up to and turn to is highly important. You may even be a mentor to someone else. Growing up, did anyone ever tell you something like: "Kids are watching," or "Kids will mimic and say whatever you do"? Well, it's true. And you might just be the someone that God will use to inspire and encourage someone else. Or, you might be that "kid" that's needing someone to encourage them. I encourage you now to find a mentor, someone who is God fearing, honest, and kind. Someone who may be doing what you want to do when you are older. Someone you admire. Be a mentor for someone. Someone to whom people can look up and be inspired. No matter what stage of life you are in,

you will always need someone to help keep you accountable
and on track with God's path for your life.

*Do you already have a mentor? Who
is that person for you?
How can you be a mentor for someone?*

Do I Have To Love My Neighbor?

like to think that I love and show love to ALL people, and, even though I have come a long way, I still have more to work on in the area of showing God's love to people. Here's what I'm seeing: I see people showing hatred to people. I see hypocritical behavior towards people. I see people excluding others.

> **"We love because he first loved us.**
> **Whoever claims to love God yet hates**
> **a brother or sister is a liar.**
> **For whoever does not love their brother**
> **and sister, whom they have seen,**
> **cannot love God whom they have not seen.**
> **And he has given us this command:**
> **Anyone who loves God must also love**
> **their brother and sister."**
> **1 John 4:19-21**

It's not until we see people through God's eyes, that our attitude and perception of them changes. Realizing that everyone has an issue, a struggle, a pain, a real life can be very eye-opening and can underline the fact that people act certain ways for a reason. I tend to ask myself this question when someone does something to upset me: What is the root of why they treated me that way? This could be a stranger or even a close friend or family member, it doesn't matter. The fact is that everyone has a soul that can be poured into and given life. Let me ask you this: What good does it do to be mean to someone? The reality is: we were all created by God. The same God that loves us also loves our enemies. We are called to do the same. Forgiveness plays a huge role here. Jesus said to first take the log out of your own eye before you try to take the speck out of your neighbor's eye (Matthew 7:3-5). In order to love others, we must first give ourselves a heart check. What are the things you need to work on in yourself that are hindering you from showing God's love to others (including your enemies)?

Next time someone does something annoying, mean,
or you think is wrong; think before you speak.
Are you showing God's love to ALL people?
What are some things you need to work on?

Words

Words can be two things: helpful or hurtful. You know that saying, "Sticks and stones may break my bones, but words may never hurt me"? Whom are we kidding?! Words stick. We listen to them, we hold onto them, and we dwell on them. People tell us words. We tell ourselves words. So, what do we really want those words to be?

> **"My dear brothers and sisters, take note of this:**
> **Everyone should be quick to listen,**
> **slow to speak**
> **and slow to become angry."**
> **James 1:19**

I often pray this verse over my day each morning for myself and those around me to be kind with our words. What we say to others and to ourselves can be life-giving or crushing to the spirit. There are so many good scriptures that talk about our words. That means it's important. The fact that words are that powerful gets forgotten daily. We do this in big, more obvious ways and in small, hidden ways. The words we say under our breath or the words spoken in a quick smirky remark after a long day have a bigger effect than we think. Think before you speak. This is something I try so hard to live by because I am someone who speaks what's on my mind. It gets me into trouble sometimes; however, seeing the negativity and sadness my words can bring to others makes me feel even worse. Guard your mouths and your thoughts. What you say to yourself in your head can be just as soul-crushing. And remember, listening to others is also powerful.

Are your words giving life or crushing the soul?
If your answer is "giving life," what effect
does that have on people and yourself?
If your answer is "crushing the soul," what effect
does that have on people and yourself?
Are you content with your answer?
How can you be slow to speak and quick to listen?

WALK THE WALK

We talked about words, now we are putting the actions to our words. When I was a youth minister, I noticed my teens were starting to transition from being a middle schooler to a high schooler and it was rough for them. We've all been there, and maybe you're remembering back to when you were that little freshman and laughing like I am right now. I had one teen in particular who had been homeschooled most of her life and was facing her first time at public school. She had many stories that sounded way too familiar but also many stories that sounded so different from how it was when I was in high school just a few years earlier. She told me the biggest issue for her at public school was that there were so many people who are not Christians. She felt constantly surrounded by people who said they were Christians, but they cussed, did bad things, and talked bad about others.

> **"Do not merely listen to the word,**
> **and so deceive yourselves.**
> **Do what it says."**
> **James 1:22**

If you're going to talk the talk, you need to walk the walk. I get it: we are human, and, sometimes, we make mistakes. However, we can say we are Christian all we want, but when our actions don't match up to what we were just saying that Sunday morning, God says it's just like looking in the mirror and then walking away and forgetting what you look like (James 1:23-24). It is not enough to read the Word of God or even go to church. We have to apply it and live it out in our daily lives. I always laughed when this girl started ranting about her new world of public school; but it made me stop and think about the people in my life who are those "Christians" she talked about and made me wonder if, sometimes, I am one of them. Words are easy to say, but actions take more effort. Actions take more of me. Actions take more time. It's worth it.

Are you walking the walk?
Do one thing this week to help another person.
Take action.

Turn The Light On

The church I grew up in has five humongous stained-glass windows all along the sanctuary. One of my favorite things was being in the sanctuary before they turned the lights on and seeing the morning sun shine through the stained-glass revealing all the bright colors. There are many different shades of blue, purple, yellow, orange, and some pink. Each one depicts a picture that represents God or a story in the Bible. Have you ever seen a stained-glass window at night? The colors turn black, the black that outlines the colors turns a dark muddy brown, and you can hardly tell what the picture is supposed to be. Once you take away the light, the beauty of the stained-glass goes away.

**"When Jesus spoke again to the people, he said,
'I am the light of the world.
Whoever follows me will never walk in darkness,
but will have the light of life.'"
John 8:12**

**"In the same way, let your light shine before others,
that they may see your good deeds
and glorify your Father in heaven."
Matthew 5:16**

Just like the stained-glass windows, when we let the light of Christ shine through us, our true beauty is revealed. Being a young adult, it almost seems strange to be a Christian. People expect us to be party goers, irresponsible, naive, etc. If anything, I want to encourage you to be uncommon. Don't be afraid to let God's light shine through you. What does that

FRANCESCA CAMPBELL

look like? It looks like being kind to <u>all</u> people and putting <u>others</u> first. It looks like having faith in hard times. It looks like pursuing God in all that you do. It looks like being different and standing out. I could go on and on, but I think you get the picture. Let God shine. That kind of light attracts people. That kind of light burns like a candle in the darkness. That kind of light is contagious. Let your light shine to glorify our Lord.

*Imagine being in a completely dark room. You can't
see anything and definitely can't move around safely.
Now imagine that you have a small
candle in that dark room.
It doesn't bring total light to every dark
corner, but it's just enough for you to move
safely and see what's around you.
Be that small candle in the darkness of the world.
Let God be that candle for you.*

How Can I Be A Servant
Of The Lord?

What is a servant? Google has a few answers that basically say a servant is someone who performs duties for another person. My favorite definition it had for a servant is a "devoted and helpful follower." The Bible talks about how we are called to have a servant's heart, and even Jesus came to this earth not to be served but to serve others. But what does having a servant's heart even mean?

> **"Whatever you do, work at it with all your heart,**
> **as working for the Lord,**
> **not for human masters,**
> **since you know that you will receive**
> **an inheritance from the Lord as a reward.**
> **It is the Lord Christ you are serving."**
> **Colossians 3:23-24**

I asked a friend one day at one of our coffee dates this question: "What does it mean to you to be a servant of the Lord?" You could tell she wasn't expecting such a question at the Starbucks on a Tuesday morning, but she had such a beautiful answer. She shared that, for her, being a servant of the Lord means being devoted to Him. It means serving Him not just at church, but everywhere you go. Such truth. She nailed it right on the head. I started to think: Yes, I want to serve the Lord in all that I do. Being a servant of God is striving with all your heart to give God glory in everything you do. I truly believe that being a servant is rooted in love. We love God; therefore, we love others (that includes everyone). It is doing acts of service and not expecting anything in return.

I love the story of the sinful woman who washed Jesus' feet with her tears in Luke 7:36-50. She dried them off using her hair, kissed them, and rubbed them with perfume. I encourage you to read the entire passage, but what I want to highlight right now is how she humbled herself before Him. The passage concludes with Jesus telling the woman her sins were forgiven. We must approach servanthood with a humble heart in order to show a Godly love towards others.

How can <u>you</u> be a servant of the Lord?
How have you seen other people in
your life be a servant of God?

Don't Hide. Go Seek.

Maybe it's just me, but when I was taking the plunge into adulthood, it was very hard for me to find other believers. There weren't any other college students–or even young adults, for that matter–at my church at the time. At college, it seemed like all the professors and my classmates were anti everything I believed in. I felt somewhat alone. I didn't really have anyone close in my life that was my age (other than my boyfriend) that loved the Lord. That was tougher than I thought it would be. I felt discouraged. I felt abnormal. I felt like I couldn't share my passions, my job (as a youth minister), or really anything about who I was. I never said anything in my classes about my faith (and there were PLENTY of opportunities to do so). I hid who I was. Because I felt like the Lord was not visually upfront in my life, I stopped seeking the Lord. The only time I talked about God was when I was at church or anytime I was confident that I was surrounded by other believers. This was so incredibly wrong.

"But if from there you seek the Lord your God,
you will find Him
if you seek Him with all your heart
and with all your soul."
Deuteronomy 4:29

Stop hiding amongst other Christians. The Lord is not confined, bound within the walls of a church building. Look for the Lord everywhere and in everything. Ask Him boldly to make Himself known in all parts of your life. Ask Him to send you people in your life that love the Lord and will help you grow in your faith. There was ONE time in one of my college classes that I actually said something that involved my faith, and I ended up finding out that there WERE several others who were just as "good at hiding" as I was. After that, we all became friends and even shared that we all felt more confident knowing that we weren't alone in the class (I still keep up with some of these girls years later). Step out in faith! Seek out the Lord and ways that you can live boldly for Him. Do not let the fear of others' rejection keep hidden the glories of God. We are called to proclaim the gospel. That means whether we are surrounded by fellow believers or not!

Are you hiding or are you seeking?
What are some things that keep you from
sharing your faith with others?

Fighting The Fight

This world we live in is so hard. Sometimes, I feel as though the world and everyone around me are against me. It's as if everything I am doing is going wrong, failing, or not even getting started. I have the feeling that I might just explode if one more bad thing happens. Yes, sometimes our battles are caused by others, and we may have no control over them; but we do always have control over how we react.

> **"I consider that our present sufferings
> are not worth comparing with the glory
> that will be revealed in us."**
> **Romans 8:18**

With every battle, we grow stronger and wiser, not because God changes the situation, but because He helps us through it and gives us a new perspective. A good way to learn how to respond to trials is to look at Jesus. He handled "hard things" with grace, kindness, love, and understanding (to name a few). That's the true test isn't it? To show grace and love in times when you feel defeated. Something I always have to remind myself of is that God sees me; He hears me; He knows what I need. I have to trust that God's going to get me through each battle. He has already won the war. Facing trials can be a good test of faith, and, with every test, we grow perseverance. I'm reminded of the story of Job. He lost all that was close to him and yet remained a faithful servant of the Lord, and the Lord blessed the latter part of Job's life even more than his former life because of his faithfulness. Let perseverance finish its work. Fight the good fight; but remember you're not alone, and in Christ there is strength beyond all measure.

Close your eyes. Take a deep breath.
May the word of the Lord be your sword.

KEEP THE CHANGE

The idea of change can be scary. Maybe because it's new, or because we fear the unknown. Are we scared of change because we feel as though we have no control? Maybe it's because we are afraid; we think we won't like it; or we worry "the change" will cause us harm. Experiencing change helps us to go beyond our comfort zones, try new things and build courage.

> **"Jesus Christ is the same**
> **yesterday**
> **and today**
> **and forever."**
> **Hebrews 13:8**

It's worth being said that in moments of change, we may need to self-reflect and realize it's not all about us (our ideas, our plans, our wants). It's not about you. Sometimes, we may have to admit that there are other people more experienced or maybe knowledgeable in the area that is being "changed" around you. Humility comes into play here. When change is happening in an area we can't control, that's when trusting in the Lord comes into play. We need to rely on Him.

It is in the moments of change in our lives where we tend to depend most on God. It is when we cry out to Him asking for guidance. Even though as young adults, we will experience many, many, many changes in our lives; the good news is that the Lord remains the same yesterday, today, and forever. Go ahead and take a leap of faith! Change can be good if we <u>make</u> it to be.

Think of a time in your life when you
went through some changes.
How did God help you during that time?
He will be just as faithful now as He was then.

Fear

There are so many things I am afraid of: snakes, mice, clowns... These aren't the kind of fears I'm talking about. I'm talking about those fears that hurt your gut, make your palms sweaty, give you anxiety, and, worst of all, hold you back from achieving your goals. The kind of fears that make you ponder for so long that you already feel defeated.

> **"So do not fear, for I am with you;**
> **Do not be dismayed, for I am your God.**
> **I will strengthen you and help you;**
> **I will uphold you with my righteous right hand."**
> **Isaiah 41:10**

Something I've noticed in myself is that my fears are often rooted in lack of control or fear of the unknown. I want to know everything before it happens, but that is hardly ever the case. Even better, there are times God calls me into circumstances that I can't even understand. This makes me feel inadequate and unequipped to do the things to which He is calling me, or to do anything, for that matter. It is time to put fear aside, move beyond our comfort zone, and let God take control. God doesn't call us to be comfortable. This verse in Isaiah reminds us that our strength comes from God: the all-powerful Creator. When we allow fear to consume our lives, we are giving control to the devil. Another thing I've learned about fear: when I walk with God through my fear, my faith grows a lot, but my fear grows little. THEN, it becomes easier and easier to step out in faith the next time fear tries to consume me.

What fears are holding you back?
Say this out loud: "I will no longer be a slave to fear!"

Prayer Works

What is prayer? We understand it to be the way we talk to God and the way He talks to us. I like to think of prayer as the stepping stones to building a relationship with God. There are many "ways" or "types" of prayer, but, ultimately, it is a one-on-one conversation with God the Father. It does not have to be long or formal; it's simply having a conversation. How and what we pray about is a personal and intimate experience; but on numerous accounts the words "pray," "prayer," and "praying" are thrown around meaninglessly. How many times have you said or has someone said to you, "I'm praying for you"? Do we really say a prayer? Have you ever had the intention of praying before you go to bed, but then you fall asleep? Do you only pray when things go wrong? Or maybe only before a meal?

> **"Devote yourselves to prayer,**
> **being watchful and thankful."**
> **Colossians 4:2**

I have this verse written on a sticky note in my office where I can always see it. It helps remind me to remember to pray. I used to be a youth minister, and the teens would always express how prayer is such a scary thing for them. They find it difficult and awkward talking to Someone who is not there physically. My number one reminder to them is that prayer is the main channel we have to ultimate love. Prayer works, my friends, and, boy, is it powerful! Pray always with intent and confidence in knowing that the Lord hears our prayers. Not only is God listening, but He is waiting for you to listen to all the things He has in store. Whatever is on your heart is important to God. Give your all to Him. Feel His presence, and pray.

My prayer life hasn't always looked the same. It changes with the seasons of my life and relationship with God. I used to rely heavily on a prayer journal. I would write down all my prayers each day. Now, I like to spend my prayer time with God saying my prayers out loud. All my prayers aren't out loud as that would be quite difficult throughout my day. But, my deep intimate prayers with God are out loud to Him. There are times when I admittingly don't feel God's presence in my prayers. Sometimes, I wonder if He hears me. I keep praying anyway. 1 Thessalonians 5:17 says to "pray without ceasing." Prayer is a lifestyle. It's a constant state of having an open mind and heart to hear and talk to God. This can be hard or even frustrating. But the more I talk to God and spend time practicing listening to Him, the more I am able to recognize His presence and His voice.

Do you feel like you have a healthy prayer life with God?
Take at least five minutes each day
or more and talk with God.

STRESS

The world is spinning, there's very little time, things are becoming overwhelming, you're overthinking every little detail—you're stressed. Stress is something I believe everyone experiences. It's okay to not be okay, but, with stress, come so many things that can negatively affect us: lack of sleep, sickness, unhappiness, a low level of self-confidence, and lack of faith that God is in control.

**"When anxiety was great within me,
your consolation brought me joy."
Psalm 94:19**

Stress is something I have fallen prey to for as long as I can remember. My anxiety is much better than it was before, but it is still a battle I face. For me, when I am stressed, I let the negative get the best of me. I tend to focus on all the things I need/want to do: whether that's putting something off for too long or having taken on too many responsibilities or trying to make a major decision. I lose focus on what God is doing in my life. Something I stand firm in when I am feeling all the pressure is that God will never give me anything I can't handle…. WITH HIM.

When my husband and I were trying to buy our first house, it took way longer than I wanted it to. It was during what they called a "seller's market," and took us over a year to even find a home we loved and that was in our price range. I was STRESSED! It consumed my mind. I was researching houses for sale constantly, praying for God to give us a house, and hating on the cute little rental house we had been in for almost 2 years at that point. I remember my stress turned into anger. I was home alone, cleaning and doing laundry. My prayer of anxiety turned into "God, why are you making this so hard?" and "Why aren't you giving us a house?" Suddenly, a shift in my heart changed. He reminded me that at least I have a roof over my head and of all the cute little things in our cute little rental house. I began to pray a prayer of thanks out loud. I was thanking God for every little thing I could think of. So as I folded laundry, I thanked Him for having clothes. I even thanked God for my pillow as I made up our bed. This prayer was giving God thanks, but if you had heard me, my tone was that of anger. Then, it shifted—not just in my tone of voice, but in my mindset; a feeling of gratitude and contentment came over me.

I use this little tool now when I am feeling stressed. Yes, I pray about the things I am stressing over, but I try to have more of an attitude of thankfulness. It helps me invite God's peace into the mix of my stress. Peace wins every time. I think, sometimes, we need to slow down and invite God into the things that stress us. Let God take back control.

*Take a moment to reflect and be
thankful for God's goodness.
What is stressing you?
What do you need to prioritize?
Come up with a game plan to tackle the things
you need to get done. Ask for help if needed!*

don't know about you, but I have a strong need for control. I am definitely a type "A" personality. I constantly try to stay motivated and feel the need to get things done. I am also a problem solver, so, when I see a need, I try to come up with a solution to fix it (including other people's problems). I am not satisfied until I feel I have done so. It drives me mad constantly thinking and pushing all the time. Always taking on new things, trying to hold everything together, maintain classes, work, be in a relationship, and have a social life is exhausting.

"He says, 'Be still, and know that I am God...'"
Psalm 46:10

Press pause, my friends. Sometimes, when we are busy and in the rush of things, we tend to forget about the One who provides peace. If you're like me, you spend a lot less time with God as things pile onto your "to-do list." I love the simplicity of this verse saying "be still"! I hear it as God saying "Just stop for a second," and the beautiful ending saying "know that I AM GOD." Wow! When these moments of silence happen for me, I am then able to see God's beauty in the things and people around me. I've learned that when I am trying to move too fast on what I think my path in life is, I tend to miss where God is leading me.

I've taken on a new interest: Minimalism. I went through a huge purge of all my things and watched many "Minimalist" videos on Youtube that talk about simplifying your life. Not only did I start to simplify my house, but I started to try to implement slow living. I learned to say, "No," and simplified my calendar. I learned to be intentional. This intentional living affects my relationships, including my relationship with God; it has affected how I spend my time and money, etc. It has been a breath of fresh air, just allowing myself to slow down. Maybe it's time to take a moment and breathe. Instead of trying to do all the things, I try really hard now to stop and ask God what He wants me to do. Know that God is in control and that He is good. He wants to help you. Press pause, and hand God the remote.

Go for a walk outside.
Try not to listen to music or be on your phone.
Hear the wind through the trees and
the birds sing their song.
Spend time with God.

Why Can't That Be Me?

My husband and I got engaged pretty young. I was 20 and he was 21. We both were still in college. We both were learning how to save and handle money, figuring out all the wonderful things of adulthood such as bills, insurance, and all those great responsibilities. (I cringe just typing it). Before and during our engagement, I saw so many young couples who were already married and had a house, amazing jobs, and two cars–blah, blah, blah... I didn't know how any of that would ever be achievable for us, for ME. Why can't that be me? How are they doing this? I can't tell you how many times I wished I could just snap my fingers and everything would just appear for me: a house, money, wedding, life... I mentioned before that I have issues with wanting control. When I want something, I do everything I possibly can to get it. But at that time, it was as if everything was right in front of me, but yet so out of reach. Do you know what I mean? It's like being a little kid who sees the cookies on the table but is too short to reach them. <u>That was my level of frustration</u>!

> **"The Lord is good to those whose hope is in Him,**
> **to the one who seeks Him;**
> **it is good to wait quietly for the salvation of the Lord."**
> **Lamentations 3:25-26**

Maybe you aren't like I was: trying to get married, find a house, graduate from college, etc. BUT maybe you are like me in the sense that it is so hard to wait for God's perfect timing. To have patience in knowing that He does have a plan for you. I tend to want things to happen NOW. It is so difficult to see other people's achievements and wait for your own. In all my struggles of learning how to be patient in waiting for God's time, one thing I have learned is that doing things on [my] time <u>never</u> works. So, if anything, I am telling you today that God is working in your favor. He knows what He is doing. I had a little joke I told myself when we were in the process of praying for God to help provide a house for us. I said it must be taking so long for Him to answer our prayers because it must be a big house. Take note, friends, that you do not have to match up with another person's timeline. Just because someone else has crossed things off their list does not make you behind in crossing things off your own. Your time line is between you and God. Let God use you as you wait.

I'm 26 now, and my husband is 27. God has blessed us with the things we once never thought would be possible. Here's a little secret: there is always going to be something that feels unachievable or out of reach to you. There is always something else you will be praying to God for and trying to be patient about. I used to think, "I'll be happy when…." That was toxic thinking. There's a lesson in contentment here. Trusting God's timing and plan for your life is hard. Being in a season of waiting is hard. With God, we can do hard things. With hard things, we grow stronger in Christ.

In your prayers this week,
tell yourself to wait patiently on the Lord.
Have faith, my friend!

Money Honey

So…I am going to give you even more a glimpse into my personal struggles. I used to (and still, sometimes) have a spending problem. I think it started after receiving several promotions and pay raises at my first job. I had no bills to pay, as I was living at home, and my parents generously blessed me. I was making a decent amount for the first time ever, and I went absolutely wild!

"Keep your lives free from the love of money
and be content with what you have,
because God has said,
'Never will I leave you; never will I forsake you.'"
Hebrews 13:5

I spent most of my money on food, clothes, unnecessary household things, and, well, more food. I think I had this problem because I love the temporary satisfaction it gives me. Being content with what I have and all the many blessings God gives me is something I am still learning. Tithing, helping others, and spending money on things I <u>need</u> are important to me now, but I never would have thought of them before. Now, I tend to ask myself, "Do I need this?" and I often tell myself, "No." It also helps me to involve other people I can trust to help me with my spending habits as well as helping me learn to be content. Ask questions! This is probably the number one thing I would tell all young adults who are learning how to manage finances. Ask the pros! Here is <u>my</u> personal answer to really cracking down on the love of money: The more I fill myself with the Holy Spirit, the less I feel a need to fill that void with STUFF. The more I pray specifically for my spending habits, the stronger I become to fight it. Money is not something we should let control our lives. Money should not be the cause of our worry, stress, or anger. Money is something we need to learn how to control.

I could go on and on about budgeting, saving, giving, tithing, investing, etc. I love learning and talking about all those things now in this stage of my life. Solomon, in the book of Proverbs, teaches us to be wise with our money, save, and give to others. He also reminds us of what I would say is the most important thing: Let God be enough for your life. Having a lot of money or things is not what makes a person truly rich. A rich person is full of the Holy Spirit.

During this week, do some research.
Where and what are you spending your
money on? Try creating a budget.
Be content with what God has given you already.

Joy

What is joy, true joy? When I was fifteen years old, my parents, younger cousin, and I lived in Costa Rica for five months. My cousin and I absolutely hated it until the last two months or so when everything started to click. We finally made friends, explored the area we lived in and LOVED the food. It was through the friends that we made that I truly saw pure joy.

Karol was the name of our closest friend in Costa Rica. My parents grew to be friends with Karol's mom, aunt, and grandmother. Karol also had two younger siblings that we let play with us older girls. Karol's brother drowned while we were there, and they could not find his body for a few days. The family was Catholic, and as part of their tradition, they had several days of wake where everyone came to their house to pray for the brother so that he would go to heaven. During this time, the family will serve food and receive flowers with many condolences. One night, my family went to one of the wakes, and as soon as we got there, Karol's family moved the couch from inside their house (where it was too crowded for us to go inside) onto their enclosed porch so we could sit down. They gave us food, and–without our knowledge–Karol was walking back and forth to the small convenience store to get more food and drink for us. She laughed with us, and we played with her younger siblings; but, finally, I stopped and asked Karol a question. I asked her, "Why are you so happy right now?" Her reply was," Because I am with you." I then proceeded to ask her about her brother and she said, "He is with God, and God is in me." It was at that moment that I witnessed true joy from the Lord.

> **"I have told you this so that my joy**
> **may be in you**
> **and that your joy**
> **may be complete."**
> **John 15:11**

This family who had nothing, who had eight to ten people living in a four-room house (including bedrooms, kitchen, and living room), who just lost a loved one–<u>they</u> are serving us?! Giving us everything they have?! "God is in me." Those words touched me to my core. True joy comes from nothing of this earth. Joy is not found in people or belongings. That joy is contemporary and we will always want more of it. Joy, true joy is found within Jesus Christ. He tells us that HIS joy will be IN us, so that OUR joy may be complete. Complete…Don't we all want to feel complete? If I have learned anything from growing up and being a young adult, it is that when I have God's joy and love in my heart, that is all I need.

Where do you find your joy?
Are you guilty of finding joy in earthly things?

Cozy

After a long day, I like to have a cup of tea, maybe some chocolate, and take a nice bubble bath and watch a movie or favorite tv show. That's probably my ideal afternoon. You know what I LOVE even more?! Rainy days. I love those rainy days when I can sit on my couch, cuddle in a blanket, read a book, watch Disney movies, and eat some comfort foods. I love all the cozy things. I make it a goal to make sure my home is warm and cozy in every season. Right now, as I'm writing this, it's close to Christmas and my favorite rainy days have turned into snow days, and my Disney movies have turned into Christmas movies, and I am LIVING FOR IT! I love to feel comfort.

"The Lord himself goes before you and will be with you;
He will never leave you nor forsake you.
Do not be afraid, do not be discouraged."
Deuteronomy 31:8

These words are comfort. Knowing that the Lord will never leave you or forsake you is freedom. He is with you wherever you go. You are not alone. As much as I love my cozy days and comfort foods, I truly feel comfort only when I rest in the knowledge that the Lord is with me and is watching over me. I remind myself constantly: The Lord only wants good for my life. With that in mind, we can find comfort in the fact that God is consistently working for our good, and He is always good. Know that the Lord sees you, hears you, and knows the desires of your heart. Take comfort in the Lord.

What things make you feel cozy?
What do you think it means to find comfort in the Lord?

FRANCESCA CAMPBELL

UNCOMFORTABLE

When you think of comfort, what comes to mind? We've talked about being cozy, how comfort can be found in a place, a feeling or in a person. Here's the problem: Sometimes, we are too comfortable. When we are too comfortable, we can get lazy; we don't want to move, get up, or take action. What happens when God calls us to be uncomfortable? When we are asked to get up and move? What happens when we are called outside of our comfort zone?

You see, we get to this place in our lives, sometimes more than once, when things are going okay. In this case, okay doesn't always equal good. What I mean is things become routine. They become familiar. You're good at something, so you keep doing it even though you don't like it. You don't like how something is going, but it's all you know, so you stay in it. Why do we do these things? Are we scared? Lazy? Untrusting of God?

Are we scared of the unknown? Are we scared of change? Are we scared we will fail? We tend to let these emotions, or lack thereof, keep us from greatness. They keep us from fulfilling God's plan for our lives. Take a look at the book of Jonah.

"Go to the great city of Nineveh and preach against it, because its wickedness has come up before me."
Jonah 1:2

Jonah was called outside of his comfort zone, and, yes, he ran away from it. But God still spared him and called him to be uncomfortable, and PEOPLE WERE SAVED! We are not called to be comfortable. We may be called to do things that are uncomfortable. Are you willing to heed the call? Are you willing to go beyond your comfort zone?

I'm going to switch gears here a little bit and ask you this question as well: Are we becoming too comfortable with God? Again, in this case, comfortable doesn't always mean good. We are comfortable with where we are or aren't with our relationship with the Lord, and we either become too lazy or too fearful to do anything about it. Are we too comfortable to praise Him with our entire being? Are we too comfortable to go deeper with God? Are we so comfortable with our routines that we lose sight of the glorious transformation that God can give when we go beyond and allow ourselves to be uncomfortable? God wants more of you. God wants all of you! We may have to go beyond our comfort with God and dive deeper into a more intimate relationship with Him.

Here's something to remember friends: We can still find comfort in the uncomfortable through Jesus Christ. Deuteronomy 31:6 says, "Be strong and courageous. Do not be afraid or terrified because of them, for the Lord your God goes with you; He will never leave you nor forsake you." God will never call you to an uncomfortable place and leave you there. That is where our comfort lies in the uncomfortable moments: Knowing that God will never leave us or forsake us.

I challenge you to be uncomfortable.
Is there something that God is calling you to
do that is outside of your comfort zone?
What's keeping you from becoming uncomfortable?

FRANCESCA CAMPBELL

LONELINESS

There are times that I have been in a crowded room and felt lonely. There are seasons when my life is full, yet I feel lonely. There are even days when I want to stay in my loneliness and days when I want to get out of it but can't figure out how. Sometimes, I don't know why I feel lonely.

I think loneliness is something everyone feels at some point in life and can hit when you least expect it. The trick is not dwelling in our loneliness. In this day and age, it feels like our world has made secluding yourself more easier to do. Between more things being available online and gatherings being made virtual, it's easy to justify keeping to ourselves. Don't get me wrong, I love being at home! I love me some alone time. I am also one to feel anxious in a large crowd or a new place. But here's the thing, we were not created to do life alone.

**"So do not fear for I am with you; be not dismayed,
for I am your God.
I will strengthen you and help you;
I will uphold you with my righteous right hand."
Isaiah 41:10**

I love how Holy Spirit connects us to God. Through Holy Spirit, we can feel God's presence and unite ourselves with Him. To me, dwelling in Holy Spirit feels like a warm hug. Many times I sit in that "hug" and just be. I let the Lord pour over me, and I feel my feelings (loneliness, fear, worry, joy–all the things I give to God) and just sit in His embrace. I know God is always with me, and I know He never leaves me; but, sometimes, I need a little bit of a push. What do we do when we feel lonely?

No matter what season you are in of adulting, it is so important to surround yourself with God-fearing people. Find your community. If you are away at college, find a Christian group on campus or make one! Find a church home. Go to church! It's not enough to watch online in your pj's. We were not created to do life alone. We need people. We need a community of fellow believers to uplift us, teach us, grow us, and keep us accountable. Baby steps. I have to be honest: people can exhaust me sometimes. I love people, and I love doing all the things, but sometimes I need a people break. I've learned that's okay sometimes, but here's what I want to share about that: keep surrounding yourself with your community anyway. Don't let your people break be too long. For me, it's a planned Saturday of doing nothing or a Sunday afternoon of strictly napping and being at home. I schedule this on my calendar.

We are in charge of our loneliness. We are in charge of how and with whom we spend our time. One small act towards breaking from your loneliness can make a huge difference. Let the Lord guide you as you walk through loneliness. Be honest with yourself, and let others in.

Have you ever felt lonely?
Do you have a community of fellow believers in your life?
If not, what can you do today to find your community?

FRIENDSHIPS

One of my favorite things to do is grab brunch or meet at a coffee shop and chat with a friend. I am really careful about who my friends are and whom to bring back into my life or not. I want friends with whom I can go beyond the surface and dig down deep. I want friends who will let me share my heart with them and theirs with me. Friends that will lift me up and point me towards the Lord. Those types of friends are sometimes hard to find. However, here is what I have learned thus far: quality is more important than quantity. It's better to have one or two faithful, deep-level friends, than a multitude of friends who only scratch the surface.

"A friend loves at all time..."
Proverbs 17:17

For the past couple of years, I have desperately prayed for God to place friends in my life who share a love for Jesus with me, will support me and let me support them, and share common interests with me. And lately, God has been seriously SHOWING UP for this once friendless girl! It has been such a joy. For the first time ever, I have those types of friends in my life. We share our faith with one another and boast in the power of God with one another. For the first time, I have friends I know I can count on. It is so important to have friends in your life. The people you surround yourself with really can touch your soul. You determine if those friendships are life-giving or soul-sucking. Whom you spend your time with can really be a reflection of who you are. Ever heard the saying, "Bad company corrupts good character"? It mentions this in 1 Corinthians 15:33 and is very true! Don't have those loving friends yet? Don't give up! Pray for them, and be patient in waiting for them. In the meantime, let God be your friend. Once you find those God fearing, amazing friends, I challenge you to dig deep. Have the hard, intimate conversations. Those are the kinds of people I want to do life with: the ones that will walk with me in my high and lows of life and not judge me.

Determine which of your friends are
really your life-giving friends.
Are you putting enough effort into your friendships?
Maybe it's time to start.
How is God our friend?

BEYOND THE MIRROR

I f you were to describe yourself to another person, what would you say? For me, I might say something like I'm tall, I have brown hair, brown eyes, tan skin, etc. I might talk about my occupation or where I went to college. But my next couple of questions get a little personal. What do you see when you look in the mirror? Are you happy with what you see? Is there something about your looks, or skills you want to change? Do you compare yourself to other people?

> **"But the Lord said to Samuel,**
> **'Do not consider his appearance or his height,**
> **for I have rejected him.**
> **The Lord does not look at the things people look at.**
> **People look at the outward appearance,**
> **but the Lord looks at the heart.'"**
> **1 Samuel 16:7**

We've all been there. We have all felt like we need to be skinnier, stronger, better looking, faster, etc. What if I told you that it goes beyond the mirror? It's the beauty on the inside that overpowers what we see on the outside. It's the kind of beauty that makes you have compassion for someone who is hurting. It's the kind of beauty that's found in a smile. It is that kind of beauty that makes you stop turning to the mirror to find your worth and validation. It's about knowing who you are in Christ and that, through Him, you can find your worth. It's about taking time to look at your heart and allow God to mold it into its true form. Confidence is knowing that the spirit on the inside will show on the outside.

Do some inventory on who you really are on the inside.
What's missing?
What do you need more of to be
beautiful on the inside?

Pour Into You

Ever since being a senior in high school, I have felt like part of my identity was pouring into others. This looked like being a mentor to teenage girls, being a Youth Leader, volunteering at church and in the community, and listening and being there for my friends and family all the time. All good things, right? That may be true, but my cup felt empty. I wanted to give more and be there for everyone, but at some point I started to resent being everything for everyone. Here's the thing. I let myself feel that way. I let myself maybe over-commit. It was no one else's fault. Where did I go wrong? I wasn't pouring into myself before pouring out to others. I was not being intentional.

**"Very early in the morning, while it was still dark,
Jesus got up, left the house
and went off to a solitary place,
where he prayed."
Mark 1:35**

Pouring into yourself looks different for everyone. For me, it's filling up my soul with God's Word. It also looks like taking a warm bubble bath, eating chocolate, and spending some good quality "me time" with myself. Maybe it's saying no to something or someone. Whatever it is, do it, and take time to pour into yourself. Just as Jesus spent time alone with God, we have the gift to do the same. When my heart is full of the Lord, I am not only able to give to others, but I am also able to recognize the ways God is calling me to give.

Wherever you are, stop and look for God in everything.
Did you find Him? Where did you see God?
Take a few minutes every day to pour
God's Word and knowledge into you.
Find something that works for you and
makes you crave the Word of the Lord.

FRANCESCA CAMPBELL

HERE I AM TO WORSHIP

W hat comes to mind when you think of worship? Some might say singing praise and worship songs on a Sunday morning at church. Some might say speaking in tongues, prayer, or meditation. There are so many different types of worship, but what I think people often don't realize is that worship is so much more.

> **"Sing to the Lord, all the earth;**
> **Proclaim His salvation day after day.**
> **Declare His glory among the nations,**
> **His marvelous deeds among all peoples.**
> **For great is the Lord and most worthy of praise…"**
> **1 Chronicles 16:23-25**

Worship is giving God glory and praise. This can be done anywhere, anytime, any place. Worship is more than a song; it's an attitude and mindset. Everything we do should be done to praise the Lord. Let me give you an example. My husband has a friend who told us that one day at Walmart he felt led to collect all the shopping carts that were randomly spread throughout the parking lot left by people who didn't take them back to the designated area. Yes, they have employees who are paid to do so, and, yes, this took him quite a bit of time. But, for him, it was a form of worship. He wasn't doing it for anything other than he felt God leading him to do it. That's worship. Colossians 3:2-4 reminds us to "set our mind on things above…." If we truly are focusing on how we can serve the Lord in all ways, then the things we do can be forms of worship to Him. Being obedient to God is worship. Showing love to others is worship. Our words, if life-giving, are worship.

I challenge you to think about ways that you can worship God outside of a Sunday morning. I invite you to find new ways to grow your worship. Do you have an attitude of worship?

How can you worship God everywhere and in any way?
When was the last time you gave God praise?

I've Got A Jar Of Dirt

Okay, let me explain… We are talking about being made new. Let me see if I can give you a visual. Get you a jar of dirt. (I instantly play back the scene in *Pirates of the Caribbean* where Jack Sparrow boastfully shouts: "I've got a jar of dirt!") The jar represents us, and the dirt represents our sin. If you were to take a pitcher of clean water and pour a little bit of it into the jar, the dirt would not go away and make the jar clean; instead, you would have dirty water in a jar. HOWEVER, if you take multiple pitchers of clean water and repeatedly pour ALL the water into your jar of dirt, the clean water will eventually push out the dirt, and you will have a jar of pure, clean water.

> **"Therefore, if anyone is in Christ,**
> **the new creation has come:**
> **The old is gone, the new is here!"**
> **2 Corinthians 5:17**

We are humans living in this world full of dirt, and we are bound to get dirt in our jar. If we constantly and consistently pour God into our jar, He will push out the dirt. The dirt that tears us away from Jesus. The dirt that causes us pain and suffering. The dirt that tells us lies. The dirt that makes us feel…dirty. "Whoever believes in me, as scripture has said, rivers of living water will flow from within them." (John 7:38) We are made new in Christ. When we say, "Yes," to Him, we are beginning the process of letting Him pour His living water into us. The key is to continuously pursue the Lord. Let's go back to the jar of dirt. Just a little bit of water started the cleaning process, but it took a continuous flow of water to push out the dirt to get a clean jar. Continuously seek after God. Pray without ceasing. Even when you don't hear an answer yet, worship Him. Even when things are going bad, seek after the Living Water, Jesus Christ. Choose God. CHOOSE GOD EVERYDAY!

If you can/want, get you a jar of dirt and truly see what I mean. (It may take a lot of water depending on how much dirt you put in and how big your jar is) How has God made you new? What's your dirt that you need to let God wash away?

My husband and my little sister credit me for being a great storyteller. I love coming up with an epic and magical bedtime story that most of the time has a theme in it to help encourage or teach you something. The story always has a purpose (other than putting you to sleep).

> **"Let us draw near to God with a sincere heart**
> **and with the full assurance that faith brings,**
> **having our hearts sprinkled to cleanse**
> **us from a guilty conscience**
> **and having our bodies washed with pure water."**
> **Hebrews 10:22**

We all have this epic story of our own—one we have lived, survived, felt, and seen with our own eyes. It's a story full of thrill, action, sadness, anger, laughter, and adventure. It's truly brilliant. The catch here is we don't always see our stories as brilliant. Our past isn't always picture perfect or something we are proud of. As a result, we add a not-so-good climax to our story: guilt. We feel guilt. We are ashamed of who we were before we started a journey of finding love in Christ Jesus. We discredit our story. God loves you and loved you through your story. He saw you; He heard you; He forgives you. He offers us redemption through Jesus Christ. Your story is worthy to be shared. It gives you a chance to brag on how God has changed your life. It makes you who you are. You become real and relatable, showing that you're only human. Tell that story of yours, friend! Release the guilt and shame you have attached to your journey. Maybe you feel guilty about things in your life now. You are never so "far gone" that God will overlook you.

You have forgiveness through Christ with repentance. Nobody is perfect. God does not call us to be perfect. God will use you. God will use your story to inspire others and to show you a different and better path He has prepared for you.

Something I have learned is God can also use your guilt. I have felt guilt many times in my life over things I knew I shouldn't have been doing. That guilt turned into conviction. That conviction led to repentance. That repentance led to freedom. Maybe God is trying to tell you something and lead you into righteousness. Don't let your guilt be a chain. Don't let it hold you back. Allow God to use it to move you forward.

Do you have guilt? About who you are?
About what you have done in the past?
Allow God to release you from your guilt.
Pray and say to God: "Free me from these chains of guilt."

Before Marriage

My husband and I were both Christians when we met. We even "courted" for 4 months before we became "boyfriend and girlfriend." My husband was much farther in his faith at the time and was so good at keeping God at the forefront of our relationship. We both agreed that God had to come first, and, if we were going to date, it would be with the intent to marry. We were all in. We were young, in love, and passionate for Christ. God truly used my husband to bring me closer to Him.

We had strict boundaries at the beginning. Most of these were physical boundaries. He wouldn't even kiss me for months because he said he thought he wanted to wait to kiss until our wedding day (that didn't last too long). We kept those boundaries pretty well for about a year, but the temptations grew. It wasn't long before those boundaries were pushed further and further, and hands started moving in places we said we wouldn't go until marriage. We ended up having sex before marriage. We justified it saying we were planning to get married anyways. We even said we were "now married in the eyes of the Lord" because we had become one physically. We told no one.

When we got married. Our sex life got worse. I thought it would get better, but it became one of the very things the devil used to tear us apart. I won't get into the details of our first year of marriage, but it was hard. We went to marriage counseling, and my husband and I told each other we wouldn't bring up that we had sex before marriage. God had other plans.

One day in our counseling session with our Christian Couples Counselor—she wasn't even talking about intimacy– as the counselor shared something intimate about her story,

I broke. We told her everything. I didn't realize I carried so much guilt about having sex before marriage. My husband and I dated for 4 years before we got married, so I had about 3 years of guilt baggage shared in that one counseling session. My husband felt it too. I'm thankful for the breaking because it brought me such freedom. I sought forgiveness, but also healing. I even confessed to my mom what I had been carrying for years, and she responded with so much grace and love. I needed that. We started to heal our marriage as well.

**"That is why a man leaves his father and mother
and is united to his wife,
and they become one flesh."
Genesis 2:24**

I tell you this part of our journey not to make you feel guilt or shame, but so you know you're not alone. We never thought we—as Christians dedicated to living a life for Jesus—would be in that position, but, man, was it hard. Society makes this even harder. Society says it's normal or even good to have sex with your partner before marriage. It's in every tv show, movie, or even song lyric glorifying sex. So how are we young adults who are striving to live a life for Christ supposed to respond?

For those of you who are feeling maybe guilt or shame, here's what I want you to know: there is forgiveness and redemption in Christ. You don't have to hold onto that anymore once you have placed it in the Lord's hands. He still loves you. I chose the verse in Genesis because I think it is a good response to the questions: "Why does God tell us to wait until marriage?" Sex is so much more than physical. It is how God intended for husband and wife to become one in flesh. One. Think about that for a second. To become one with another person. That is why sex is so important. It's fun, it feels good, but there is a spiritual side of this form of intimacy that God intended to be for husband and wife. I encourage you to wait. It's also not too late to be abstinent again.

For those of you who are struggling, like we were, to uphold the physical boundaries in your relationship, I see you. Talk about it. Talk about your struggles with your partner. Talk about your boundaries again and again. Maybe you don't need to sit so close to each other on the couch. Maybe you don't need to share a blanket where hands are hidden and free to wander. Maybe you don't need to be left in a room alone. Maybe don't take a long drive and park somewhere. You know your limits. I encourage you to not be the "average adult" that society tells us young adults should be when it comes to relationships and sex. If I were to go back and give past Francesca advice, I would tell her not to keep her sin hidden. I would tell her to not hold onto guilt but to seek after God daily and pray to Him about sex. God can handle those conversations. Sex [true intimacy] is worth the wait.

For those of you who are single, navigating dating, and wanting to wait to have sex until marriage: wait on the Lord. Your value is not found in any one of anything (or act). Your value is in Him. Male or female, waiting to have sex is HARD. Don't let society tempt you. Sleeping around or "testing the waters" is not going to bring you fulfillment. Masturbation is also not going to satisfy you or bring you fulfillment. Fullness only comes from the Lord and that my friends is why sex is worth the wait. Give your desires to the Lord. Pray and ask how God can use you in your singleness. Find your worth in Him not in the bed sheets.

Do you find it hard to refrain from having sex or doing other things that could lead to sex with your partner? What are some boundaries you need to put in place?

Grace Upon Grace

Why are we so hard on ourselves? Oftentimes we are our own biggest enemy. We can be the greatest wall that stands in our way of reaching our goals, chasing our dreams, being confident and feeling the joy of the Lord. I, personally, have quite the inner critic. This voice in my head is constantly bringing me down and causing me to doubt everything I know to be true. My toughest battle within myself is struggling to feel "good enough." Am I doing the right things, making the right choices, doing enough? Will I ever be good enough? Where do all these pressures come from?

> **"For the grace of God has appeared**
> **that offers salvation to all people."**
> **Titus 2:11**

Here's the thing: God knows we are human, which means He knows we are going to make mistakes. Psalm 103:8 tells us: "The Lord is compassionate and gracious, slow to anger, abounding in love." It's okay to make mistakes. Learn from them. There's always going to be someone we think is better than we are. There's always going to be more to do and ways to become "better." But it is God's grace that frees us from our strict to-do list. It is by His grace we have salvation. By His grace, we have hope. By His grace, we have love. By His grace, we have joy. By His grace, we have mercy. By His grace, we have Jesus Christ. <u>Give yourself grace!</u> In case nobody has told you lately: You're doing a good job. Cut yourself some slack. Take it one step at a time and recognize all the good you have done and are doing. Give yourself permission to slow down, reflect, and realize you don't have to have it all together.

In what ways do you need to give yourself grace?
Reward yourself with something you love:
coffee, time with friends, a cheeseburger!

Printed in the United States
by Baker & Taylor Publisher Services

Printed in the United States
by Baker & Taylor Publisher Services